D0742387

CHILD MADE
OF SAND

ALSO BY THOMAS LUX

MEMORY'S HANDGRENADE, *1972*

THE GLASSBLOWER'S BREATH, *1976*

SUNDAY, *1979*

HALF PROMISED LAND, *1986*

THE DROWNED RIVER, *1990*

SPLIT HORIZON, *1994*

THE BLIND SWIMMER: SELECTED EARLY POEMS,
   1970–1975, 1996

NEW AND SELECTED POEMS, *1975–1995, 1997*

THE STREET OF CLOCKS, *2001*

THE CRADLE PLACE, *2004*

GOD PARTICLES, *2008*

FROM THE SOUTHLAND (NONFICTION), *2012*

CHILD MADE OF SAND

THOMAS LUX

Houghton Mifflin Harcourt

Boston   New York   2012

Copyright © 2012 by Thomas Lux

ALL RIGHTS RESERVED

For information about permission to reproduce selections from this book,
write to Permissions, Houghton Mifflin Harcourt Publishing Company,
215 Park Avenue South, New York, New York 10003.

www.hmhbooks.com

Library of Congress Cataloging-in-Publication Data
Lux, Thomas, date.
    Child made of sand : poems, 2007–2011 / Thomas Lux.
      p. cm.
    ISBN 978-0-547-58098-2 (hardback)
    I. Title.
    PS3562.U87C48 2012
    811'.54—dc23   2012014033

Book design by Patrick Barry

Printed in the United States of America

DOC 10 9 8 7 6 5 4 3 2 1

Many of the poems in this book first appeared in the following publications: *American Poetry Review:*
"Outline for My Memoir," "Why," "The Goldfish Room (Where the Cops Beat You in the Head
with a Phonebook)," "Lady's Slipper," "Graves Rented by the Hour," "Hatrack," "Since Death
and Its Sequelae," "Dendrochronologist Blues." *Cortland Review:* "The Probabilist," "Fox," "Like Tiny
Baby Jesus, in Velour Pants, Sliding down Your Throat (A Belgian Euphemism)." *Dossier Journal:*
"The Chairman of Naught." *Field:* "The Moths Who Come in the Night to Drink Our Tears,"
"The Hunchback Farmhand." *Mead:* "Rue de la Vieille Lanterne," "Not the Same Kind of Mud as in
'Two Tramps in Mud Time.'" *Ploughshares:* "The Queen of Truth," "Elegy." *Plume:* "Soup Teachers."
PoetryMagazine.com: "From Whom All Blessings Flow," "A Delivery of Dung," "The Drunken
Forest," "You and Your Ilk." Poets.org (Academy of American Poets): "Dead Horse." *Smartish Pace:*
"The Underappreciated Pontooniers," "The Riverine Farmers." *Southampton Review:* "The Little
Three-Handed Engine That Could," "*Scriptus Interruptus.*" *Terminus:* "A Frozen Ball of Rattlesnakes,"
"Nietzsche Throws His Arms Around the Neck of a Dray Horse," "The River of Nuts." *Toadlily Press:*
"West Shining Tree." *TygerBurning:* "Every Time Someone Masturbates God Kills a Kitten."

for Jennifer Holley

Mundo cosi, cosi.
(Such, such is the world.)
—ANTONIO DE SOSA,
Diálogo de los Morabutos

Write! Comrade, Write!
—EMILY DICKINSON

Joy, shipmate, joy!
—WALT WHITMAN

CONTENTS

CHILD MADE
OF SAND

I

THE MOTHS WHO COME IN THE
NIGHT TO DRINK OUR TEARS

always leave quenched,
though they're drinking,
in composition, seawater,
which does not make them insane
as it does parched humans when we
drink it, even
with our big, big bodies.
If you knew
a leper's tears do not contain
the bacillus *leprae,*
would you let him weep on your chest?
Let the moths come, let the sandwoman and -man come,
let Morpheus and Dreamadum come
unto me, and my beloveds,
let the moths come
and drink of the disburdening waters.

THE LITTLE THREE-HANDED
ENGINE THAT COULD

I give the engine an extra hand, one more than Milton
gave his in the lines from "Lycidas":
But that two-handed engine at the door/
Stands ready to smite once, and smite no more.
Scholars disagree on the exegesis
of these lines: the dual-edged sword
of the archangel Michael? the two houses of Parliament?
death and damnation?
I'd say they're each right, as right
as right is possible,
and add: There's a man at the door
and he wants to kill you!
I've given him an extra hand — two to smite with swords
and one to smite, as well, with a dagger.
Have you ever tried to read "Lycidas"?
No wonder Robert Lowell, manic
as a buzz saw, tried to rewrite it!
It's a hard haul through our early tongue
and there are at least 17 references/allusions
in each of its 193 lines.
I read it all morning and I read it all night.
The next day all day
and 100 miles into the dark.
I still understand little,
and care little about his quarrel with the clergy;
though I am sorry for the loss of his friend
Edward King, drowned in the Irish Sea.

But there is a symphony
in my garden now, the air is a symphony all around me,
the river, the trees,
there is a symphony
in blind, blind Milton's poem
in my hands! Oh,
I'm on a little train
cresting a hill and my engine
is a symphony, and also its smoke.

The Chairman of Naught brings his forehead to the table
and three wax apples tremble
in a blue bowl, though no one
except the Chairman
is here. Profits are down,
but no one can tell him how much.
There's a pie chart (he loves pie charts!)
on a whiteboard, as yet undivided, unequally.
It's an uncut pie chart pie.
This one's only a circle,
a porthole, the little round *lunette*
of the guillotine. Profits are down,
the Chairman says, way down.
I'll have to let some of you go.
To go: there's nobody, nobody here to go.
The Chairman checks his tie — it's tight.
The boardroom's lighted by everyday light.

YOU AND YOUR ILK

I have thought much upon
who might be my ilk,
and that I am ilk myself if I have ilk.
Is one of my ilk, or me, the barber
who cuts the hair of the blind?
And the man crushed by cruelties
for which we can't imagine sorrow,
who would be his ilk?
And whose ilk was it
standing around, hands in pockets, May 1933,
when 2,242 tons of books were burned?
So, what makes my ilkness *my*
ilkness? No answers, none obtainable.
To be one of the ilks, that's all
I hoped for; to say hello to the mailman,
nod to my neighbors, watch
my children climb the stairs of a big yellow bus
that takes them to a place
where they learn to read
and write and eat their lunches
from puzzle trays — all around them, amid
the clatter and din,
amid bananas, bread, and milk,
all around them: them and *their* ilk.

THE DRUNKEN FOREST

—for Ilya Kaminsky

When the permafrost
begins to melt
and all the trees lean
this way and another: Russians
call it a drunken forest.
A forest, in Russia,
usually means Siberia, the *taiga,*
and it was in Siberia,
in Vladivostok, a place in the pit
of a wind-stabbed continent's tip,
on December 27, 1938,
Osip Mandelshtam died
(of cold, no food)
and did not die.

Without their work building bridges,
armies, for centuries, were stopped
by rivers as fast and deep
as their need to cross.
Dragging animal bladders, planks,
dismantled boats . . . The ranks
part to let them pass so they can reach
the river and its banks and start
to do their art.
Amid stones and arrows (*like black needles,*
some whistle) they build their pontoon bridges,
sometimes with rowboats spaced across a river,
pontooniers rowing furiously in place,
upriver, boards laid across their rowboats,
over which their harquebusiers and pikemen rush.
When all have crossed the pontooniers wait
and guard their threads
from this shore to that, they wait
for their engineers to come to build
a bridge of stone, or steel.
Then to chase their armies' dust again!

NIETZSCHE THROWS HIS ARMS AROUND
THE NECK OF A DRAY HORSE

and it signals the beginning of his final breakdown?
An act of empathy — as if he felt how broken
that broken horse was? He could. Or
was it tertiary syphilis? Unlike
many philosophers — rigid,
tortured by the abstract — it was the concretions
that broke Nietzsche. Were the electric drills
of his migraines physiological,
or did he think too hard
and know not, well enough, how to be loved, or to love,
like most of we?

He sat in his chair: *scritch, scratch, tappety-tap.*
There were pronouns, many pronouns: you
and her, he and she, though rarely they,
and a minimum of I. That was important: a minimum
of I, since I is always there.
Nouns, lots of nouns, the "dense thing-ness" of them.
Love nouns, they make the world!
Scritch, scratch, tappety-tap,
some noises nosing around other noises.
Not too many adjectives, a scantiness of adverbs,
those lazy parts of speech, softer
than the thump of a dog
hit by a dump truck, in fog,
two blocks away. But the verbs,
when active — talk about dancing!
An image here, a simile there,
say one thing and mean another.
It gave him pleasure, even when
he wrote with blades and rage,
even when he left nothing on the page
but slash marks, even when all he did was play,
sometimes ably, ofttimes less so,
with others, others far and others close.

A FROZEN BALL OF RATTLESNAKES

How'd they get in a ball?
What do you mean by a ball, how many in it,
and do you mean stone-frozen?
Or do you mean dormant, sluggish, half hibernating?
Snakes can do that, right?
Rattlesnakes live in other countries too.
There are many species, right?
I'd seen copperheads and cottonmouths
in some mountains
and a few desultory streams I knew.
I live in a large southern metropolis now
and my neighbors
found a rattler (albeit a small one) in their cellar.
Killed it with a shovel.
They have a child, and a dog.
In the frozen ball, do they wake up one by one?
Are those closest to the middle
warmer than the others?
They're all cold-blooded.
Lincoln used the phrase, metaphorically, more than once.
It's a good metaphor, easy to read, vivid. Metaphors
should be, and sometimes
should terrify: A man chops
off another man's head, props
the corpse sitting up against a roadside pole
and places the man's head in his hands,
on his lap.

If torture is the Queen of Truth
then what is the King of Truth?
Could it be the Black Dog, ennui,
accidie? Can the King
rule by the weight
of the ink (oh, I pray
not the pixels!) on an execution order?
Could the King be numbed by dumdum fever?
Could the King be a thug, theocratic or not?
Might the King's epiphanies be arsenic-lit?
Can the King pass his edicts
from behind a screen?
Maybe not so Long Live the King!
What kind of King passes the torture off
on his wife? Please. Please, Your Majesty,
step up, show us you've got something new!
Something well past torture.
Something long, and slow, and cruel.
The King, outranking the Queen,
who resorts to torture *alone*
to obtain the truths she needs, the King
with his funny hat and ruffled collar,
what can the King do
(let's find out)
that hasn't already been done by the Queen?

interrupted Wordsworth as he drafted "Intimations of Immortality."
A timely wagonload
if one considers only
the title. An honest man knows
there is no such thing — immortality — hints or no hints.
I prefer Wordsworth the Younger,
his early/mid-thirties, when the abovementioned
was written, when he and Dorothy
still had most of their teeth
and before he was spoiled (milk-sopped,
and walking like an alderman
fed on too much turtle soup) by Dorothy (sister),
Mary (wife), and Sara (sister-in-law), and sometimes even another
Sarah (Coleridge's wife, estranged).
Wordsworth the Elder
obtained a sinecure selling stamps,
wrote many bad poems,
lived a long, honorable life, and,
truth is, he *is* immortal,
or as close as a corpse can get, would be
immortal for the first four stanzas of "Intimations"
alone. *Those stanzas alone.*
Anonymous — "Western Wind" — achieved the same with four lines!
No piece of art is perfect.
All it has to do is stay around

for two hundred, or five hundred,
or a few thousand
years. It (art) always changing; us,
not so much.

II

ELEGY

— *César Vallejo, Arago Clinic, Paris, Holy Friday,*
   April 15, 1938

It was you, César, they killed to the base of your forefinger, you.
Certainly they shot Pedro Rojas too.
No doubt Juana Vásquez was killed.
The killers, poor also, were skilled.
And Emilio, they shot him in the back of the neck
after they made him kneel amid the wreck
of his grandmother's house — they beat
but did not kill her. The people, their hands and feet
(*A cripple sleeps with his foot on his shoulder.*
Shall I later talk about Picasso, of all people?),
these are the people you wrote for, César,
though your later poems, no longer lighted by the laser
of your homeland, of *Heraldos Negros* or *Trilce*,
were real enough for exile but not as true, licit.
Socialist realism, the aesthetic was called,
poetry force-marched — to diminish, equally, all.
It was not right for your mind and betrayed your heart.
Your countrymen and -women should bring you home, César.
Entombed in France is good enough for some,
but Peru should bring Peru's great poet home.

are works in progress
and not finished until nature says so,
I will linger on it no more;
neither will I argue for nothingness
(I read about twenty pages of that nauseating book once
and considered shooting myself in the head
until I remembered I was a pacifist
and had given away all my guns), nor argue for an afterlife.
I'm not going to whine about there being no God,
or if there is a God what a sadistic ditz He is;
the sound of a body bag's zipper won't buzz my ear;
nor joy run through me, nor fear.
I shall not lament that, without consciousness,
I'll no longer enjoy the thought
that Descartes favored cross-eyed women,
or that each year elvers, or glass eels, ascend our rivers
and pass their mothers — silver eels — descending seaward.
Tell me yellow fever rages
and mosquitoes breed in the nave's
holy water: I won't blink.
Nor will I ever, *ever*
gripe again that we're all going to the same place
but won't be seeing each other there!
I'll never say: I'll die before I pay
a window tax; being at peace,
I'll get over it, never mention again

how unhappy I'll be when the world's gone from me
and I'm excused from want and want and want.
It doesn't concern me a peep,
and, in fact, *I'll have no more on't.*

EVERY TIME SOMEONE MASTURBATES
GOD KILLS A KITTEN

Why not kill a rat? There're lots of rats! Remember
the time You gave some of them fleas,
which killed them (that was good), but then the fleas jumped off
the dead rats
and bit humans,
who died too, about a third of them
on the planet? You *were*
good to Poland (hardly any occurrences), which You
made up for in following centuries.
How about snakes? Why such vituperation?
Little whips, You made, with such racking poison!
How about clams? Would one clam feel the loss
of another clam in, at least, a version of grief? I'm not sorry,
I prefer clams to rats or snakes.
I eat clams, but I'm willing to never
eat a clam again — for the kittens.
How about You,
how about adjusting Your plan
a little, how about a little less hard-ass?
How about You tell Your flock it's time to let this bill pass?

WEST SHINING TREE

West, but west of where?
How far west? Northwest, southwest?
I need to get there, un-iambically.
Please send coordinates.
Longitude and latitude, please.
Why is it shining? That affirms light, life,
though west also associates with death,
which also affirms life — if you're not dead.
What kind of tree is it? Leafy? Tall?
Hardwood, fever tree, balsa?
A tree of luminous fruit?
In prose, it's evening light through a tree,
looking east to west.
May it be more: an emblem,
a synthesis of something beyond
another sundown on the back lawn
under the retractable awning.
I want to stand beneath this tree.
I want to put my hand to its bark.
I'll leave tonight, no, Tuesday.
I'll head dead west and ask of all I see:
Which is the way, the long or the short way,
to the west shining tree?

Whom says: *Here's a tomato. Slice it.*
You do: one side rolls left,
the other right, and both
show you the chambers
of their split hearts, their slippery liquids,
and seeds,
which you take, eat,
because of their abundance.
Across a small pond
a boy squats by the edge
stirring the water with his hand.
His father's five strides behind,
too far to stop him if he topples face-first.
The water is black but shallow.
It's been eons since alligators lived here.
The boy falls forward.
The best, or the worst, that can happen: his father,
laughing, lifts him by the seat of his pants,
two seconds submerged,
from the water. A family joke, or,
for the boy, shame
and a lifelong distrust of water. Thanks, Whom.
Nobody ever sees Whom around.
Whom gets credit
for what Whom never lifted a pinky

to do, or not to do.

Whom doesn't have, I don't think, a pinky.

Nor do I think Whom would know what to do with it
if Whom did.

THE PROBABILIST

Maybe I'm tergiversating about it: do
I want to lie there, waxy, mute,
and hear neither weeping nor laughter?
Maybe? The *Current Subject*
has no brother or sister of the full
or half blood. I'm not sure
it will arrive at that, but if it does
most likely afterward there could be
a casserole at Aunt Mina's.
Aunt Lily could be there with her famous kugel!
All of my dead might be there.
Mother? Father? The *Current Subject*
has no brother or sister of the full or half blood.
I guess it could possibly
maybe come to that.
Probably I should just stand here and take it
like a man, probably.

RUE DE LA VIEILLE LANTERNE

— *Gérard de Nerval (1808–1855)*

Where are the shoelaces of yesteryear, Gérard?
Those with which you hanged yourself
from a streetlamp? Or, as some accounts say,
from a window grating, on this little rathole
street in Paris, where there's a plaque for you.
Perhaps "window grating" is less poetic in French.
Some called you an early, though not the last, *poète-maudit.*
A poet who walked a pet lobster on a blue leash
seems, however, hardly glum!
Some kind of hide, I'm assuming shoelaces
in the nineteenth century were stout
and long enough to wrap around
your neck a few times.
An early walker of a French dog,
is that who first discovered you, Gérard,
or the last drunk stumbling home?
The shoelaces of yesteryear, where did they go?
The same place as François Villon's snows
of yesteryear, nearly four centuries before you took exit,
the same place as the snows of last winter, and all the winters
in between, and all snows to come.

LIKE TINY BABY JESUS, IN VELOUR PANTS, SLIDING DOWN YOUR THROAT (A BELGIAN EUPHEMISM)

— Jenny

It tasted so good; the touch of it tasted so . . . God,
handless, must have had a hand in it; it wasn't "like" anything,
though language without simile is like a lung
without air, or air and nary
a lung to breathe. It was like the lip
of a small waterfall, its perfect curve,
the half-breath-held-split-moment
the last few inches of horizontal river
turn into the first few inches of vertical river.
It was like that, or, it was like, but better than,
the word "negligee" or the word "nugatory"
or "lagniappe" (pronounced *lan-yap:* a small gift or tip).
It was, too, like the color of the crow's wing,
in which blue and green burn beneath the black.
I'd compare it to a perfect parabola,
at the exact peak of which
a man shot out of a cannon exclaims: Yes!
I'll land dead center of the net,
let's move the cannon back
twenty feet, increase the powder load, redo the physics,
let's try it again *right now!*
It felt like holding an otter intent
on play, it was like a ptarmigan
on the tundra guarding her eggs,
it was like the moon in the glass eye

of a man lying in the grass
but not like the moon in his good
eye — that's a little puff of cataract.
No, it was not like, nor unlike, anything.
It was her heart carving
the air as she spoke.

NOT THE SAME KIND OF MUD AS IN "TWO TRAMPS IN MUD TIME"

The dust motes of mud at a pond's bottom,
sluggish river, or swamp. The finest, most ethereal
of muds, rising in soft pinheads
from the density below; the fog of mud, what first
grips your ankle so whisperly, a little warmer
than the water above it, a satiny sock
saying, *Dip your foot a little deeper into* . . .
The mud of blur and smudge.
The almost drinkable mud.
The dusk of mud, the passage, the membrane,
the place between less creamy mud
and harder mud, riverbed.
Drifty elixir, reenvisioning
us, red-carpeting us, down.

ERMINE NOOSE

Mink runners up the thirteen steps, mink
the hangman's hood
and black marten his gloves. The priest's cassock
mink, his crucifix chinchilla, each hair combed
to catch dawn's yellow light, his black book gilt-bound.
Some can choose
(pay for) the noose
to be softened, lined
with ermine,
but when the floor door's latch unsnaps
they drop
as sharply as anyone,
or more so: softer nooses tighten faster.
A comic in the crowd
holds a lifeless mouse by its tail
(or might that be a baby mink?),
which he tosses
into the open grave
in the graveyard
adjoining the gallows' ground.

WHY

> It is an execrable and damnable monosyllable,
> why; it exasperates God, ruins us.
> —*John Donne, Sermon CXXX*

Why so much bread rotting on shelves and the mice so fat they roll
to their holes
at night, their legs too short
to pass their bellies to the floor, whyzat?
What starts up the diphtherial winds, melanoma sunsets?
I was also wondering (*So he stood in his shoes /
And he wonder'd. / He stood in his shoes / And he wonder'd.*) why
the years come to resemble a greasy deck of cards,
why afternoons bleed,
why does my friend die
before I've met her in the flesh
which she ordered turned to ash
the minute she was dead?
Now that I'm asking: Why the incapables, thirsty
at the lip only, why
the incapables commanding the capables,
and howzit the broken, melon-kneed horse
is made to kneel
before the bullet to his brain?
I'm full of whys!
Why is there no limit to recrudescence?
Why did that man jump so high
he forgot to come down, why, in a place with no more air,
it still *looks* as if air remains,
why-o, why-o, why?

III

OTHER VOICES

MADSONG

Jebus don't love me, oh.
Oh Jebus don't love me, no.
He never because I too slow.

The moon do love me, but it fall,
plash, way there in ocean
where I see them small
fishes who be, who be a ton

of teeth in my big eyes. So,
Jebus, let this tiny haminal go,
because I don't love you neither, no.

Farming by a river, your fields
within twenty feet of its bank's shade trees.
Drinking from the river,
bathing in it, feeding your fields with its waters,
taking fish and, in winter, eels
from beneath the ice
at its crenelated edges,
thanking it for the silt it leaves after spring's snowmelt,
sitting by it in August when it's lowest,
its bigger bed-stones exposed. . . .
What we'd do, because there was a bow
in the river, what we'd do — my brothers
and I — was launch some boats of sticks
and leaves and race across the bow's neck
to see which ones made it
around the bend's swirling eddies,
then watch them ride the little rapids
that slid under the barbwire fence line
ending our land. The boys
sometimes threw stones at the boats,
making boy-noise explosions.
Father stood at the river's edge,
one hand in his pocket,
the other leaning on the walking stick
he needed. On the wind,

a quarter mile upriver, Mother was weeping.
Every year the river. Every year the weeping.
Every year the sowing,
most years the reaping.

We're against it, the moon, we don't like it up there,
always a threat to fall on us! It never
holds still, it never
stays the same shape — every night
it's somewhere else, and growing
from a fingernail clipping
to a dinner plate,
which is too bright.
And other anomalies too.
It can't be trusted.
We're lobbying hard against it.
More people, afraid to speak out before,
join us every night.
We don't care what the poets say,
or the astronauts, nor even Priestess Luna.
Priestess Sub-Luna we call her,
and her minions we call forelock-tugging,
slipper-licking lackeys! We're going to haul it down,
the moon, we'll slap its face,
excise it from the sky.
We demand darkness, darkness every night,
and when the moon
is dust we'll start to extinguish, too,
the stars.

PENULTIMATUM

I put forth, in this document, two demands
that are *almost* ultimatums.
I'm sending it to you now
to presage the ultimatum, along shortly,
if you do not
grant them: I want bowls,
a spoon by each, set up on long tables
in a large room, in front of empty chairs,
chairs once occupied by war orphans,
empty because there are no more war orphans!
I want, also, diminished: amputations,
multiple, in partic., I'm *almost*
demanding the number of lost limbs
not exceed more than one, singular,
a one-limb limit. That's all
I'm penultimating
now. I hope you will please
consider these.
(It would be a start.)
Or: Oh, then, then will come the ultimatum.

One half inch long, mother-
of-pearl handle, slim, sharp steel blade.
X-rays: a tiny knife
in this baby's brain, raised
at an angle — as if leading a charge up and out
his fontanel. The baby's fine,
he's a fat baby,
and already sleeps all night
on a belly full
of his mother's milk.
Will it hurt my baby? It's his twin,
the doctor says, I can take him out.

GRAVES RENTED BY THE HOUR

The dead can't afford much rest,
they've got to do
the business of being dead, fast,
and climb out. The mourners
are all out searching for their own graves.
Somebody heard a man got nine days
(five consecutive, sundial included) in one of the hill towns.
Nobody likes to be buried
up there — the wind never stops
and it blows hard enough to lift gravel — but
in times like these . . . The good thing is the price is
stable; in fact, it's dipping
in a few places (the aforementioned hill towns)
and in some parts
of the wet
and weedy
lowlands.

DENDROCHRONOLOGIST BLUES

I don't like cutting down big trees,
the two-, three-thousand-year-old trees.
When one falls on its own
it's usually sick inside,
and if that sickness runs its whole trunk's throat
I can't do my work: to count its rings
and read each one — we can do this — for drouth years
or cold, or no sun, which year the locust, the years of bark mites,
the years of war (minute
grains of gunpowder and blood), famine (tooth marks),
Eighteen Hundred And Starve To Death (1815),
the years of many marryings and births, sun
and rain and food in equipoise.
We can know the ingredients
of the air, the soil. We can tell
the years we were not here at all,
or when there were, of us, fewer.
So we cut the old trees down
and saw the best six to eight feet from the trunk,
just above where its roots' tendons
strain to hold it straight.
Then we saw them into disks
an inch or two thick.
We let the rain and the stars
interpret the stump. Once,
the whole crew, wet and tired, got drunk
and played a game of poker

using the huge and ancient disks as chips.
Back at our lab, with calipers
and chemicals, with things you would not understand,
we read the world, from where it's been to where it's going,
until it's time to enter the forest again
and apply the saw to the ankles
of another great, great, great, garrulous ancestor.

THE GOLDFISH ROOM (WHERE THE COPS BEAT YOU IN THE HEAD WITH A PHONEBOOK)

No way I rat, I don't care a row of red apples,
I've been at the wrong end of sharper things; I've been hit in the head
by harder things. A diamond anvil
once, the flat
of my mother's hand,
a shovel, pickax
(that time my face was on fire); there was the bus
backed over my head.
My skull still pliable enough
the doctor molded it back (this was the 1940s) to almost
normal. By my third arrest
for literacy
the cops knew I was a bum case. I said: If
you hang me, do it high enough
so the wolves can't eat,
at night, my feet.
They gave me a choice: rubber hose
or the Yellow Pages.
I said: The Yellow Pages, so afterward
I can look up bulldozers,
so I can look up acetylene and stones,
so I can look up your address,
so I can look up salt to sow . . .
I've been hit harder, heavier, with this object

or that word,
by people who *didn't care*
(which *did* scare me)
what gashes, what lacerations, were left.

THE RIVER OF NUTS

We'd go there, my family, and our people,
after the prickly pear season
and our bellies were full
with its fruit. Our Aunties began to talk
of the River of Nuts. Their noses
telling them: oil, protein,
ripe the first day
after the four-sleep trek to get there.
We walked and walked, I was thirsty, I cried,
my mother hit me with a stick.
The River of Nuts, she said, keep walking.
The last hill (your people call it a mountain) was the hardest.
From the top we saw the river, first alone
across a brown plain, then disappearing
into denser and denser trees.
They looked *huge.*
Once beneath them, they were God. (Whom you call God
we call Mother Sky.)
The trees dropped some of their gifts
and more fell with every breeze.
We children laughed when one of us
was hit on the head or shoulder. It hardly hurt.
Uncle Shut the Bleep Up* said he'd heard of pinecones
big enough to kill you when they fell,
or make you ugly with scars. We told Uncle: _____ ____ _____ __!
Your people call this nut the walnut.
A stupid name, walnut.

That's something we'd call a barren, a no-food
place. We call it: The Nut
Mother Sky Gives Us After She Gives Us the Prickly Pears
and Before We Follow the Great Herds,
Which She Gives Us — for Meat, Bones, and Hide.
Now: it's the River of Nuts! The river itself
is smooth and cold, its pools thrashing
with trout. Nuts and trout, nuts and trout,
our lucky life there
at the River of Nuts
when I was a girl.
How many centuries since then?
The centuries during which
I'm glad I did not live?

---

* In our culture, we avoided the overuse of what you call four-letter words, not because
they offended us, but because they were clichés. The only consequence for abusing these
words was the possibility of acquiring a nickname like Uncle Shut the Bleep Up.

BABY MADSONG

A pony's a pony because he didn't eat his oats.
The puppy won't be a dog unless she eats her bones.
A snakelet never a snake if humans don't moan.

It's best to be good, but often not bad to be bad.
Daddy, Mommy won't die, and neither will you.
You can weep, or wail, but it's better to laugh.
Grammy, Grampy won't die, and neither will you.

Walk down to the river and get in your boat.
Don't fear sleep, don't fear waking, and know:
the river takes you where it wants to go.

IV

HATRACK

He was tall and skinny, my friend,
and my father called him Hatrack.
Hatrack's father, my father's friend,
my father called Pipecleaner.
Pipecleaner called my father Rabbit,
after Rabbit Maranville, who played 23 years
in the big leagues and made the Hall of Fame
after 13 tries. Everybody
had another name: Benny the Bum,
Cowboy (he had 19 children), Two-Finger
Looey (he had all his fingers),
the Bread Twins: Crumby and Crusty.
My pals had aka's too: Zip, Feato, Monsoon, Bombo,
Bags. They called me Luxy,
which makes sense, but lacks the aplomb
of my father's friends' — *all*
of whom he outlived — or my friends' nicknames,
only one of whom, Feato, is dead.
It was his heart, I heard,
of which he always lived in dread.

FISHING

What I liked about fishing was this: you read
what you couldn't see by holding a line
between your index finger and your thumb.
There was an *S* of a worm, thrice-pierced,
on a hook at the line's end, and
on the other end, in your other hand,
a reel and a rod. The slightest
tightening of the line, an inch sliding
forward — oh, I liked that!
What was it down there nosing
the worm — the pale,
now drowned worm — what was it
down there but the tactile, tactile, tactile?
A clot of leaves could fool you, or a stick
underwater, though not for long: if it was a fish
the line bumped, or almost buzzed.
I went to a small brook, equipped as above,
a hundred or two hundred times,
and caught enough fish, total, to feed a few barn cats,
twice. I had a friend, though, who could toss his line
in the same brook's pools and hook
a fish by the belly, tail, wherever
he wanted, if it did not bite his worm.
He could feel the fish through the hook's end and its barb's tips.
He could caress its flanks, and when he snapped his wrist
the fish was his, which he did not release, but ate,
that night, dredged in a little flour and fried in butter

in an impressive cast-iron skillet, which his father,
a few years before my friend was born,
once dropped on his foot
and broke three toes, which was the cause
of his limp, not the war he fought,
and jumped from airplanes
into the terrible night skies.

SOUP TEACHERS,

we called them, the women who stood behind
the cafeteria counters
and dished it out: fish sticks, undocumented meat, soup.
War widows, then wives of the war-wounded,
then the women
who worked in war industries,
of whom my mother was one,
got first dibs on these jobs.
It wasn't a law, my father said, it just was.
My father was deferred
for reasons of agriculture.
During another war, I too was deferred,
for reasons other than agriculture.
Though short-listed for Soup Teacher,
my mother took another job
that better suited her soft
and sonorous voice: she was the one,
when you picked up the phone,
who said: Number, please.
She lost that work when dials came in.
Her voice was sweet
but she couldn't sing,
so she used it less and less
(my father was mostly deaf)
until she never spoke three syllables
in a row again.

THE HUNCHBACK FARMHAND

He got that way, said the man who hired him,
by hunching over rows
to do what I hired him to do: hunch over rows,
twist a stem — beans, squash — and snap it off.
His broken back
bends downward
and to the left. He ate
with us at the picnic table,
leaning on his higher elbow,
after the hay was in,
during which he was little
help: he could lift a bale but not heave it above his hump
onto the flatbed truck.
In a good year, hay's second mowing
is the season's last, so
he'd stay until all the eating was done
and then walk home,
the back way, through the woods,
on a path he knew,
two miles shorter
than by road.

LADY'S SLIPPER

Cold country orchids: in woods I walked knee deep in snow
they'd make a show
in spring, though not in profusion,
in modest groups of two or three.
If they were people, people'd say: They keep to themselves,
but that time our barn caught fire
they were the first . . . It was against the law
to pick a Lady's Slipper,
though you weren't likely to: they're drab, their mouths
splotched with drained purple,
their petals and sepals greenish.
Stubby, stolid, pinch-fisted. Considered vandalism
to step on one, even by accident,
meant censure in our village, and to mock
or crush one with purpose
put you in the ducking chair.
Whenever I went to the woods,
especially with my cousin Cliffy (who liked to shoot
at light aircraft with his .22), my father
or Cliffy's father would say: Don't step on no Lady Slippers!
And watch out for the quicksand
in those boggy acres
below Underwood's Hill.
When I was your age, but smarter,
a horse and wagon
sunk there once.

BRICKS SINKING IN DEEP WATER

At what depth does their dull orange disappear?
I rowed out to where I know the water's deep,
and in my rowboat a cargo
of bricks, fifty balanced
across the stern, just so.
At the bottom of this reservoir
was a town. Two towns, in truth.
Its people were paid an honest price
to leave, but no question: they had to move.
I anchor my boat forty feet above
what was once a pasture.
I take a brick from port first
and hold it by its upper right corner
and dip its lower left corner into the water
before I let it slip my fingers.
The next one I take from starboard,
but drop from port, and so forth and on.
It's the *sinestre* hand that does the work.
I never counted two seconds before one was gone
from touch, and sound, and sight. They sink until they stop
on now drowned and grassless land.
Why do I want to leave a small scattering
of man-made triangular stones
at the bottom of this no-bones
(the cemetery relocated)
body of water? In darkness, who does not love
the faint, hard, orange glow
of building bricks?

DEAD HORSE

At the fence line, I was about to call him in when,
at two-thirds profile, head low
and away from me, he fell first
to his right front knee
and then the left, and he was down,
dead before he hit the . . .
My father saw him drop, too,
and a neighbor, who walked over.
He was a good horse, old,
spavined, eating grass during the day
and his oats and hay
at night. He didn't mind, or try to boss, the cows
with which he shared these acres.
My father said: Happens. Our neighbor,
named Malcolm, walked back to his place
and was soon grinding toward us
with his tractor's new backhoe,
of which he was proud
but so far used only to dig two sump holes.
It was the knacker who'd haul away a cow.
A horse, a good horse, you buried
where he, or she, fell. Malcolm
cut a trench beside the horse
and we pushed him in.
I'd already said goodbye
before I tried to close his eyes.
Our neighbor returned the dirt

from where it came. In it: stones,
stones never seen before
by a human's, nor even a worm's, eye.
With the back of a shovel
we tamped the dirt down.
One dumb cow
stood by. It was a Friday.
For supper we ate hot dogs, with beans
on buttered white bread. Every Friday,
hot dogs and beans.

FOX

My father said: Fox took another chicken last night
and scared two others to death,
and your goddamn dog never lifted his head.
Kill it. He meant the fox,
not the dog. I followed his tracks
and the small splats
of blood and brown feathers
through the snow (I was glad
it snowed, I couldn't track a moose
on dry ground) to his foxhole
near the top of a steep hill
about a half mile away; fresh, loose
dirt marked it easy among some small pines.
I knew not to go too near
and leave my scent,
so set up a good shot thirty yards away.
I built a small wall of snow, tripodded my rifle.
When he comes out of his den again
I shoot the red fox dead.
Two hours later,
I hear my father call: Fox took another chicken!
I moved neither my blue finger
from the trigger nor the crosshairs
off his foxhole. Turns out, he had a back door.
In no foxhole I'd ever seen or heard of — in movies,

comics, TV shows, school, and later, in books,
did a foxhole have a back door; no, only one door,
upward, through the roof—a helmet usually—over which,
and through which, bullets and shrapnel tore.

A WALK IN THE WOODS WITH SHOTGUNS

Three or four of us, in a line
(we were always
in lines!), entering the woods
behind the local ball fields to hunt
squirrels, grouse, maybe get a shot at a crow.
Of varmints, they were the maestros.
That's how Fish and Game
classified them: varmints,
meaning you could shoot them year-round,
were almost obliged to, if you — fat
chance — could.
During pheasant season
we'd be walking fanned out
across a broken cornfield.
In deer season *I* wouldn't
be entering these woods: too many rifles,
long-range, shoot anything, half-drunk
big guns, .30–30s, buckshot, deer slugs . . .
Maybe I slowed up, or stumbled
a little, or the guy behind me stepped
on a pebble or a twig
and the left barrel
of his 12-gauge side-by-side went off
while its right barrel
was even with, and an inch from, my left ear.
The load was #8 birdshot.
On my cheek I swear I felt the heat.

If the pebble, or the angle of the twig,
were skewed another way
and parts of my brain
preceded me into these woods . . . ?
I didn't remember the guy's name.
He was a year or two younger
and not a regular hunting buddy.
Forty-something years later,
walking with my daughter near my parents',
her grandparents', house, a man
on his lawn called out to me: "You're so-and-so (I won't
use my own name
since this is already autobiographical enough)
and I nearly blew your head off!"
We chatted. His last name is Burt: he has a sign
on his lawn's lamppost: Burt's Barn.
My parents had a similar sign: The Luxs.
(I can't forgo my patronymic in this case.)
They are dead now
and I am not.

OUTLINE FOR MY MEMOIR

The time my horse got stuck in the mud.
(Two paragraphs; no, one.)
Went blind in right eye, took some medicine,
I could see again. Scary detail: when the doctor
first shined the little light
into my pupil, he drew back, startled.
(Three paragraphs.) Later, high school: broken heart.
(Since this happens rarely, milk for three, four
paragraphs.) *Milk,* speaking
of which: I helped my father peddle it,
in a square white truck in a small round town.
College, my twenties: I recall little to interest you.
I did cover many pages with writing,
and read, and turned a thousand
pages for every one on which I wrote.
(Don't see how I can say what else happened then
and be honest.) My thirties? Wore funny glasses.
(Maybe a two-sentence self-deprecatory joke?)
My forties, fifties? The best part
was a child, named Claudia. I could say some funny
things about her, but so could every father.
Besides, family is personal, private, *blood.*
(With above exception of daughter, those two decades:
a paragraph, maybe two if I insert
journal entry on day of her birth?)
I can't bear to write of her mother, whom I hurt.
Lately? Read like a hungry machine,

in a new room, in a house I love; there is still
my child to love, and friends,
and a beloved, named Jenny.
My vital signs are vital.
I tend a little garden, have a job.
(No way I could write more than a few sentences
on these years
under the sentence, again,
of happiness.) If I live a hundred lives,
then I'll know more truths, maybe, and lies,
to write *my* memoir, novella-sized.